# Cool CANDY Crafts

PIL Publications International, Ltd.

**Amy Belonio** has an MA in art education and has taught art for five years. She is also a freelance designer and a very busy mother of two.

**Melony Bradley** is a full-time freelance craft designer/professional and a member of the Craft and Hobby Association. She lives in the small, picturesque town of Hernando, Mississippi, where she is continually inspired to create.

**Barb Chauncey** is a craft designer who has contributed to several magazines and books, including *Quick-Sew Denim*. She teaches art to elementary-school students.

**Sharon Miller Cindrich** is a writer, craft designer, and contributing editor of *FamilyFun* magazine. She is the author of *E-Parenting: Keeping Up with Your Tech-Savvy Kids* and has contributed to *FamilyFun Birthday Cakes* and *FamilyFun Fast Family Dinners*.

**Helen L. Rafson** is a longtime craft designer whose designs have been published in numerous books and magazines. She specializes in kids' crafts, recycled crafts, and seasonal crafts.

**Photography:** Peter Rossi/PDR Productions, Inc.

**Photo Stylist:** Lisa Wright/Redbird Visuals

**Food Stylist:** Kim Hartman/Modern Amalgamated Duo, Inc.

Copyright © 2007 Publications International, Ltd. All rights reserved. This book may not be reproduced or quoted in whole or in part by any means whatsoever without written permission from:

Louis Weber, CEO
Publications International, Ltd.
7373 North Cicero Avenue
Lincolnwood, Illinois 60712

Permission is never granted for commercial purposes.

ISBN-13: 978-1-4127-1488-4
ISBN-10: 1-4127-1488-5

Manufactured in China.

8  7  6  5  4  3  2  1

# CONTENTS

# CANDY CRAFTING

Whether 8 years old or 80, everyone loves candy. While candy is fun to eat, it's also fun to use in crafts—and there are so many ways to get creative with it! Looking for something to keep the kids busy on a rainy day? Perhaps it's your turn to lead a classroom project, or you need a creative activity for the scout troop. No problem! *Cool Candy Crafts* has something fun for everyone.

This book offers a calendar year's worth of projects that are exciting to make, great to give as gifts, and best of all, tasty to nibble. In *Cool Candy Crafts,* an educational bookworm helps kids learn their ABCs, springtime robins cheep for worms, and yummy mummies make for a happy Halloween.

The simple candy crafts in this book require craft materials, many of which you probably already have on hand. A few of the crafts involve simple oven or microwave use. Each project includes a list of instructions and materials needed. Take the time to go over the instructions for each project carefully, and be sure you have all the materials on hand before getting started. Here are a few of the basic materials that are required for some of the projects in this book:

**Oven or microwave:** When using an oven or microwave, be sure children are supervised at all times.

**Knives:** Directions may ask for something to be cut out, and a knife may be the best choice. If young children will be working on the project, we recommend they use a plastic butter knife. It may be safe for older children to use a metal knife (not a steak

or paring knife, though), but you best know your children's abilities. And even with a plastic knife, it is recommended you always supervise the children's work.

**Low-temperature glue gun:** When using a glue gun, be sure children are supervised at all times.

**Scissors:** If you are using scissors to make a craft that will be eaten, be sure the scissors are washed and dried before use. Also, use appropriate scissors for the child's age. Round-tipped scissors are a better choice for younger children.

**Smock:** Be sure children wear smocks or old shirts to protect their clothes while working with paints, food coloring, and other messy materials.

## Pattern Perfect

A few of the projects featured in this book include patterns to help you complete the craft more

easily. When a project's instructions tell you to cut out a shape according to the pattern, photocopy the pattern from the book, enlarging it as directed. Trace the pattern from the copy onto whatever material the pattern directs, using a pencil.

## Decorating with Icing

We have recommended using food storage bags as pastry bags. They are inexpensive and disposable, which makes them great tools for classroom and scout projects. If you are decorating the candy craft projects yourself to hand out to kids, then you may want to consider using pastry bags, couplers, and pastry tips to decorate the crafts. These tools will create a more professional and polished look.

Some children will be able to complete the crafts with little help, but there will be times when your assistance is needed. Other projects just need a watchful eye. It's best if you and your child review the project together and then make a decision about your role.

All of the projects in *Cool Candy Crafts* are meant to provide children with a fun, creative outlet. But don't be hemmed in by the instructions—use our projects as a jumping-off point for your own unique crafts! Dream up any number of changes: Use different colors or materials, or embellish the craft any way you want. There's no limit to what you can come up with!

Completing the projects in this book should be an enjoyable, creative, educational, and energizing experience for children. Encourage them to use their imaginations, don't forget to praise and admire their results, and above all, enjoy the valuable bonding time spent with them.

# BRILLIANT BOOKWORM

*What better way is there to share a love of learning than with this bright and colorful bookworm?*

## What You'll Need

Candy: 5 small peppermint patties, mini candy-coated chocolate pieces, rope licorice (yellow, green), green fruit leather
Canned chocolate frosting

Scissors
Toothpick
Pencil
Tracing paper

**1** Use frosting to attach mini candy-coated chocolate pieces to peppermint patties. Make a "B" on first patty, "C" on second, and "D" on third.

**2** On another peppermint patty, use chocolate frosting to create eyeglasses. Place 2 orange mini candy-coated chocolate pieces in glasses to create eyes. Dab chocolate frosting in center of each eye for iris. Cut a short length of yellow rope licorice for mouth, and attach below glasses with frosting.

**3** To make antennae, cut two 1¼-inch pieces of green rope licorice. Using toothpick, poke 2 holes in top of patty head. Insert 1 antennae end into each hole. Apply dot of frosting to back of 2 chocolate pieces; place 1 at end of each antennae.

**4** Line up head, undecorated peppermint patty, and "B," "C," and "D" patties.

**5** Cut out enlarged book pattern with scissors. Use pattern to cut 2 books from green fruit leather. Press books together and attach to undecorated patty with frosting. Use frosting to attach red mini candy-coated chocolate pieces to make "A" shape on book. Attach brown chocolate pieces with frosting on each side of book to create hands.

*Enlarge pattern 200 percent.*

# CUPCAKE CONE ROCKETS

*These ice cream cone rockets are out of this world!*

## What You'll Need

Candy: striped white and milk chocolate candy kisses, round
   gummy candies, round sugar candies, gumdrops
24 flat-bottom ice cream cones
1 package (18¼ ounces) cake mix, any flavor, plus ingredients to
   prepare mix
18 chocolate wafer cookies
Serrated knife

1 Preheat oven to 350°F. Stand cones upright in muffin cups.
Prepare cake mix according to package directions. Place
about 2 tablespoons batter in each cone. Bake about 18 minutes
or until toothpick inserted into center comes out clean. Place cones
upside-down on wire rack.

2 Place 2 gummy candies on flat bottom (now top) of each
cone. (The heat from the cone will melt candy slightly and
make it stick.) Place chocolate kiss or gumdrop on top of gummy
candies. Decorate sides of cones by holding candy discs against
warm sides to resemble buttons. Let cones cool completely.

3 Cut each cookie into quarters using serrated knife. Cut four
thin slits through thick rim of cone using small sharp knife,
spacing slits evenly around cone. Slide cookie pieces in slits to
secure.                                       Makes 24 cupcakes

**Note:** *Adult supervision is required when using microwave or
oven.*

**Hint:** *If cones cool too quickly to melt candies in place, place
¼ cup chocolate chips in a small resealable storage bag. Do
not seal; place in microwave. Heat at medium (50%) 2 to 2½
minutes or until melted. Seal bag and squeeze melted chocolate
to one corner. Cut off corner and use melted chocolate as glue
to attach candies to cone.*

# Yummy Mummy Suckers

*Yarn-wrapped lollipops are adorable, easy-to-make mummies!*

## What You'll Need

Candy: oblong lollipops
White yarn
Craft glue
Wiggle eyes
Orange cardstock

Decorative scissors
Hole punch
Ribbon
Black marker or computer
    printer

**1** Wrap yarn from top of lollipop to approximately ⅓ way down stick, leaving a small opening for eyes near top of lollipop. Secure yarn ends with glue. (Glue will come off when wrapper is removed.) Glue wiggle eyes into yarn opening.

**2** Write or print phrases on cardstock. Cut 1×2-inch tags from cardstock with decorative scissors. Punch hole in tag, and loop ribbon through hole. Tie around stick.

### Suggested Phrases:

Mummies Love to Wrap

Too Cute to Spook

Eat, Drink, and Be Scary

Have a Haunted Halloween

Boo from the Crew

No Tricks...Only Treats

# *Spooky Spiders*

*These spiders are fun and inexpensive Halloween party decorations.*

## What You'll Need (per spider)

Candy: 8 tube-shape
   candy rolls
Black craft foam
Scissors
White marker

Wiggle eyes
Foam glue
Low-temp glue gun, glue sticks
Adhesive-backed foam letters

**1** Draw and cut out 4½-inch foam circle for spider body. Draw and cut out two 1¼-inch foam circles for eyes.

**2** With marker, outline body and eyes. Draw mouth in center of body. Using foam glue, glue wiggle eyes to foam eyes; glue foam eyes to top of body.

**3** To create legs, use low-temp glue gun to attach 4 candy rolls to each side of body, gluing wrapper ends to body.

**4** Adhere stickers to spell "EEK," "YUM," or other short words.

**Note:** *Adult supervision is required when using glue gun.*

# TOM THE TURKEY

*Here's a tasty turkey you can gobble right up!*

## What You'll Need (per turkey)

Candy: caramels, candy corn, chocolate chip, mini candy-coated chocolate pieces, red rope licorice

Nonstick foil
Peanut butter
Dark-colored food coloring
Cotton swab

**1** Melt 5 caramels in bowl in microwave. Pour melted caramel into round puddle on foil. While caramel is still warm, arrange candy corn feathers and a chocolate chip beak to form turkey.

**2** Apply peanut butter to back of 2 mini candy-coated chocolate pieces, and place above chocolate chip for eyes. Dip cotton swab into food coloring, and dot on mini candy-coated chocolate pieces to make pupils.

**3** Cut a 2-inch piece of licorice. Use peanut butter to attach licorice piece to chocolate chip as turkey waddle. Cool turkey completely before removing from foil.

**Note:** *Adult supervision is required when using microwave.*

# HANUKKAH HARD CANDY HANGERS

*Celebrate the Festival of Lights with a sweet decoration that will brighten any room!*

## What You'll Need

Candy: assorted hard candies (blue, yellow, white), decorative sprinkles
Food storage bags

Small hammer
Ribbon

**1** Preheat oven to 350° F. Line cookie sheet with foil.

**2** Place hard candies in separate food storage bags by color; use hammer to break candy into pieces. (Use whole or broken candies, depending on design.) Arrange candies into desired pattern on cookie sheet.

**3** Bake for approximately 5 minutes or just until melted. Cooking time will vary, depending on candy and oven. Do not overbake! Remove from oven.

**4** To add hanging holes, puncture with end of spoon while candy is still warm. Press decorative sprinkles into baked design. If candy hardens before finished, briefly reheat in oven.

**5** Let design cool on foil. Carefully peel candy off foil and add ribbon hanger.

**Note:** *Adult supervision is required when using oven.*

# HOLIDAY ELF

*Kids will love to nibble on—and play with—this adorable little elf!*

## What You'll Need

Candy: white hard candy
  circles, red fruit leather,
  small round candy,
  red rope licorice

2 white chenille stems
Scissors

**1** Hold chenille stems together; fold in half. Open back up and insert both stem ends through hard candy circle. Place candy at fold to create head. Twist chenille stems to secure.

**2** Pull a chenille stem to either side and twist each into small loop at end to create hands.

**3** String 4 candy circles onto 2 middle chenille stems to create body. Separate stems to hold body in place; at each stem end, attach a candy circle to make feet.

**4** Cut small triangle from fruit leather with scissors and shape into conical hat. Press round hard candy to top of hat. Stick hat firmly to top of head. Cut 2 lengths of rope licorice; tie around elf's neck for scarf.

# CANDY CANE

*This simple craft puts a new twist on a classic holiday treat!*

## What You'll Need

Hard candy circles, 14 each
  red and white

2 large white chenille stems

**1** Twist both chenille stems around a hard candy circle to secure end of candy cane. String candies on both chenille stems, alternating colors.

**2** At end of stem, twist stem over last candy to secure. Gently bend to create candy cane shape.

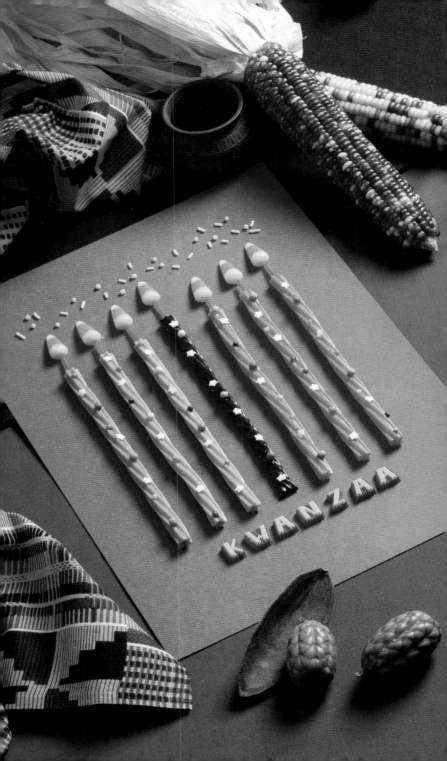

# KWANZAA CANDY KINARA

*Kids can celebrate this harvest holiday with a "glowing" kinara candleholder.*

## What You'll Need

Candy: licorice sticks (green, red, black), red rope licorice, candy corn, decorative sprinkles, candy letters
Construction paper or colored plate

Knife or scissors
Almond Royal Icing (see page 47)

**1** For candles, cut 1 inch off top of 3 green and 3 red licorice sticks. Use an entire black licorice stick. Apply icing to one side of each licorice stick to attach to plate or paper; place vertically in order to create candles: 3 green, 1 black, 3 red.

**2** Cut red rope licorice into small pieces to make wicks. With icing, attach a wick to each candle, and top with a candy corn flame. Add sprinkles around each flame, attaching with icing.

**3** With icing, attach sprinkles across candles and add candy letters to spell "Kwanzaa."

# 100 SWEET DAYS

*Celebrate your child's first 100 days of school with this eye-catching craft!*

## What You'll Need

Candy: 100 jelly beans
Foam numbers: two 0s, 1
Acrylic paint
Paintbrush
Craft glue
Spray gloss sealer (optional)

3 mini eye hooks
Ribbon
Scissors
Student and teacher photos
Cardstock

**1** Paint foam numbers. Glue jelly beans onto numbers. Spray with sealer, if desired.

**2** Glue eye hook to top of each number. Thread ribbon through each hook; tie bow at top.

**3** Trim photos to size. Glue photos to back of 0s, with photos facing out through openings. Cut cardstock to fit back of each number. Glue cardstock to back of ornaments.

**Note:** *This project uses nonedible materials—do not ingest! Adult supervision is require if using sealer.*

# FROSTY FELLA ORNAMENTS

*These holiday ornaments are full of festive fun!*

## What You'll Need (per ornament)

Candy: large marshmallows,
   gumdrop, jumbo round hard
   candy, mini candy canes,
   orange candy sprinkles, red
   rope licorice
Clear plastic cup
Scissors or awl
12 inches ribbon, ¼ inch wide
4 beads to match ribbon
White foam sheet, 1 inch thick

Pencil
Serrated knife
White wax candle
Sanding block or sandpaper
Rickrack
Craft glue
Toothpicks
Black decorating gel
Fine icing decorating tip

**1** Have an adult punch a hole in bottom of cup with scissors or awl. Thread ribbon through hole. Tie end inside cup into large double knot. Thread beads through ribbon on outside of cup. Tie ribbon in double knot, leaving loop on end for hanger.

**2** Trace rim of cup on foam sheet with pencil. Have an adult cut out circle with serrated knife. (Rub knife with wax candle to make it glide when cutting.) Sand edges of foam until circle fits securely into cup.

**3** Cut a piece of rickrack to fit around top of cup and another to fit around foam circle; glue in place.

**4** Thread 2 marshmallows on a toothpick. Use decorating gel to attach gumdrop to top of round hard candy to make hat. Attach hat to top of marshmallow snowman with gel.

**5** Cut off hook ends of candy canes; stick a candy cane in each side of bottom marshmallow for arms. Make eyes and mouth with black decorating gel, and attach orange candy sprinkle for nose. Tie rope licorice below face to make scarf.

**6** Stick a toothpick into middle of foam circle; place snowman on toothpick to hold in place. Glue foam into bottom of cup.

# Cupid's Candy Arrows

*Show that special someone you care with this sweet valentine.*

## What You'll Need (for middle arrow)

Candy: 10 hard candy circles (red, pink, white), candy letters, mini round candies, heart-shape candies
Glue
2 chenille stems
Adhesive-backed craft foam, assorted colors

Scissors
Red craft wire
Pencil
Assorted beads: red, white, pink
Ribbon

1 Glue hard candy circles together in a column, using different colors to form a pattern. Keep holes free of excess glue. Lay column on side. Twist 2 chenille stems together and push through center of column.

2 Cut adhesive-backed craft foam into 2 arrow tips and 6 Vs for arrow feathers. Sandwich stems between 2 arrow tips and 3 sets of arrow feathers, placing arrow tips at one end and feathers at other end.

3 For hanger, wrap wire around pencil; pull off. Twist one end of wire around stem near arrow tip. String assorted beads on wire. Twist free wire end onto opposite end of stem. Tie or glue ribbon to top of hanger.

4 Glue candy letters to candy column. Decorate arrow ends with assorted candies.

**Note:** *This craft is not edible. For an edible version, see below.*

## Imagination Station!

You can make this an edible treat with a few substitutions. Use icing instead of glue and candy straws instead of chenille stems. To make arrow tip and ends, use chewing gum.

# Lucky Layers

*Easy to make and pretty to look at, this pot o' sugary goodness will be a surefire hit!*

## What You'll Need

Candy: yellow candies, small green lollipop
Decorating sugars, candy powders, gelatin powders, or drink mixes (assorted colors)
Empty baby food jar

**1** Pour candy powder or sugar into baby food jar, one color at a time, layering for rainbow effect.

**2** Top off with a golden treasure of candies. Include a green lollipop to dip into sugar.

**Hint:** *To intensify powder's color, add a few drops of food coloring and stir.*

### Imagination Station!
Try using different colored sugars and dyes to celebrate other occasions. For example, use red, pink, and white for Valentine's Day!

# Robin Redbreast and Friends

*Celebrate spring's arrival with these sweet "tweets"!*

## What You'll Need

Candy: shredded chewing gum, small blue egg-shape candies, ball sprinkles, large and small chocolate eggs, taffy (red, yellow, brown), red rope licorice

Almond Royal Icing (see page 47)

1 Arrange shredded gum into nest shape; fill with small blue egg-shape candies.

2 Create 2 birds' eyes by adhering ball sprinkles to chocolate egg bodies with icing.

3 Mold red taffy into oval for robin's red breast. Shape yellow taffy into beak and feet. Make 2 wings with brown taffy. Cut a piece of rope licorice for worm; place in robin's beak.

4 Using icing, attach bird parts to chocolate egg body.

# EASTER SHAKERS

*Whether for an Easter basket or a classroom, fill these shakers with candy for a fun holiday treat!*

## What You'll Need (for bunny)

Paper
Black fine-point marker
White craft foam
Cardstock: dark pink, light pink
Scissors
Ruler

2¼×4-inch candy favor box
Craft glue
White embroidery thread
Wiggle eyes
Ribbon
Small candies

**1** Trace enlarged patterns onto dark pink cardstock and cut out. For head, cut 2-inch circle from foam. From light pink cardstock, cut two ¾-inch circles for cheeks. From dark pink cardstock, cut ½-inch circle for nose.

**2** Outline edges of box, foam, and cardstock pieces with marker.

**3** Glue inside ears to outside ears, and glue ears to back of head. Glue cheeks and wiggle eyes to face. For whiskers, cut three 3-inch lengths of thread and glue to face; glue nose on top of whiskers. Glue hands and feet to front of box.

**4** Tie ribbon in a bow and glue to front of box. Fill box with candy.

*Enlarge patterns 200 percent.*

*Cut 2 each.*

### IMAGINATION STATION!

Try making other shaker animals. To make a baby chick, paint the box yellow, cut out triangles for a beak, and add feathers. Let your imagination run wild!

# MOM'S JEWELRY BOX

*This Mother's Day show Mom you treasure her with this jewelry box full of sweet sparklers.*

## What You'll Need

Candy: 5 large white chocolate candy bars, candy letters and decorations, candy necklaces and bracelets, ring lollipops, candy lipsticks

Almond Royal Icing (see page 47)

1 Cut or break a candy bar in half width-wise. These will be the short sides of box.

2 Construct box by laying a full candy bar flat; attach side pieces (2 full and 2 half bars) with icing. Hold in place until icing is firm. Use icing to attach decorations to outside of box.

3 Fill box with candy jewels. Create one-of-a-kind jewels by icing together different candies.

4 Use icing to attach remaining full candy bar to box at an angle for lid.

# BIRTHDAY VASE

*A colorful flower vase makes for an unforgettable birthday gift!*

## What You'll Need

Candy: candy sticks, jelly beans
Glass cup with straight sides
    (no taller than candy stick)
Low-temp glue gun, glue sticks
Ribbon

Hole punch
Tag
Flowers

**1** Glue candy sticks around glass cup. Glue jelly bean border around top and bottom of vase.

**2** Tie ribbon around vase. Punch hole in top of tag; thread ribbon through hole. Tie ribbon in bow. Fill vase with festive flowers.

**Note:** *This craft is not edible. Adult supervision is required when using glue gun.*

**IMAGINATION STATION!**
Want to make a vase for Halloween or the Fourth of July? Experiment with different colored candy sticks to adapt this craft to any occasion.

# DADDY'S DAY BAIT BUCKET

*Show Dad he's the best catch with this fishing pail of yummy sweets!*

## What You'll Need

Candy: candy letters, gummy worms and fish, white chocolate candy bar, red lollipops, small disk candies, licorice sticks, red rope licorice

Small tin pail
Almond Royal Icing (see page 47)

1 Use icing to attach candy letters to front of pail.

2 Fill pail with assorted gummy creatures.

3 Melt white chocolate candy bar in bowl in microwave. Dip top half of lollipops in chocolate to create fishing bobbers. While chocolate is still wet, place small disk candy on top of lollipop. When chocolate is set, cut stick off lollipop.

4 Fill hole in top of licorice stick with icing. Push end of rope licorice into licorice hole to make fishing pole. Tie gummy worm or fish to end of licorice line.

# CLOWN LOLLIPOP

*Kids can express their creativity with these wacky lollipops!*

## What You'll Need (per clown)

1 lollipop, 5½-inch diameter
Plastic wrap
Tape
Pencil
Scissors: regular, pinking shears
Cardstock: yellow, orange, red, white, black
Jumbo star punch

Black fine-point marker
Craft glue
White acrylic paint
Paintbrush
Black narrow rickrack
Seam sealant
Pom-poms: 1½ inch, six ¾ inch
22 inches ribbon, ⅞ inch wide

**1** Remove plastic covering from lollipop, and wrap in plastic wrap. Secure ends around stick with tape.

**2** Trace patterns onto cardstock. Cut out shapes, using pinking shears for hair.

**3** Using star punch, punch 2 stars from yellow cardstock for cheeks. With black marker, outline cheeks, mouth, and eyeballs. Glue an iris to each eyeball. Paint highlight dots in irises with white paint.

**4** Cut 3½-inch piece of rickrack; apply seam sealant to ends. Glue to mouth. Glue mouth, cheeks, eyes, hair, and 1½-inch pom-pom for nose to lollipop. Glue ¾-inch pom-poms to hair at head.

**5** Wrap ribbon around lollipop stick and tie into a bow. Cut ribbon ends in V, and apply seam sealant to ends.

*Enlarge patterns 200 percent.*

# CANDY COOKOUT

*Summertime is even sweeter with this lip-smacking picnic!*

## What You'll Need

Candy: assorted colors square candy chews, caramels, chocolate turtle, taffy (orange, yellow, green, white, pink, red), green fruit leather, assorted candy sprinkles, red squeezable candy gel, small yellow pastel candies, red candy fruit slices, white bone candies
Board
Almond Royal Icing (see page 47)
Small plastic cup

**1** To create blanket, use icing to attach candy chews to board in checkerboard pattern.

**2** For hamburger, shape caramels into 2 bun halves. Shape chocolate turtle hamburger patty, cheese-shaped orange taffy, and green fruit leather lettuce. Assemble hamburger; top bun with sprinkles for sesame seeds.

**3** To make french fries, cut yellow taffy into strips. Drizzle candy gel on top for ketchup.

**4** Assemble corncob by attaching yellow pastel candies to yellow taffy with icing. Wrap with green fruit leather husk.

**5** Make watermelon slice by layering small green taffy pieces to bottom of fruit slice. Attach sprinkles for seeds.

**6** Assemble chicken bucket by molding strips of alternating white, pink, and red taffy candies to outside of cup. Mold chicken legs from caramels. Insert bone candies into an end; place in bucket.

**7** Create trail of ants by using icing to attach ball-shaped sprinkles to blanket.

# PEANUT BUTTER CUP CRITTERS

*Springtime means all sorts of critters come out to play!*

## What You'll Need (for one of each)

Candies: fruit leather (yellow, green, blue, red), peanut butter cups, candy wafers, decorating gel (white, black), mini candy-coated chocolate pieces, red rope licorice

Canned chocolate frosting
Plastic knife
Ruler
Toothpick

### BUMBLEBEE

1 With plastic knife, cut six $1/4 \times 2 5/8$-inch strips of yellow fruit leather. Press 2 strips together; repeat to make 3 stripes. Press stripes on top of peanut butter cup. Trim excess leather.

2 To create wings, cut candy wafer in half. Apply chocolate frosting to back of wings and place onto bee.

3 Use white decorating gel to make eyes. Dot black decorating gel in center of eyes.

### TURTLE

1 To create legs, cut four $1/2 \times 2 3/8$-inch strips of green fruit leather. Press 2 strips on top of one another; crisscross under turtle to make 4 legs.

2 For head, cut two $3/4$-inch circles from green fruit leather. Press leather pieces together.

3 Using toothpick, apply frosting to back of legs and head and attach both to upside-down peanut butter cup. Cut $3/4$-inch piece of green fruit leather to make tail. Apply chocolate frosting to end of tail; attach to bottom of turtle.

**4** Make 2 eyes on head with black decorating gel.

**5** Apply frosting to back of 5 green and 4 yellow mini candy-coated chocolate pieces; place on back of turtle.

### LADYBUG

**1** For body, cut two 2-inch circles from red fruit leather. Press circles on top of each other. Cut ½ inch off an edge of fruit leather and place on top of peanut butter cup.

**2** Use frosting to attach one side of 6 brown mini candy-coated chocolate pieces to body for spots.

**3** Use white decorating gel to make eyes. Dot black decorating gel in center of eyes.

### FISH

**1** For body, cut two 2-inch circles from blue fruit leather. Press circles on top of each other. Cut ½ inch off an edge of fruit leather and place on top of peanut butter cup.

**2** Cut two 1½-inch triangles for tail and ⅞-inch triangles for fins from green fruit leather. Press 2 tails together and 2 fins together. Attach fin and tail to fish with frosting.

**3** Use chocolate frosting to attach 6 orange mini candy-coated chocolate pieces to fish.

**4** For eye, dot black decorating gel on center of yellow mini candy-coated chocolate piece. For mouth, cut ½-inch-long piece of red fruit leather. Attach both to head with frosting.

## MOUSE

**1** To create ears, apply chocolate frosting to bottom of pink candy wafers. Place ears on peanut butter cup.

**2** Use white decorating gel to make eyes. Dot black decorating gel in center of eyes.

**3** Use frosting to attach brown mini candy-coated chocolate piece for nose.

**4** Make hole in center back of peanut butter cup with toothpick. Cut 3½-inch piece of licorice for tail; insert tail in hole.

**Note:** *If the fruit leather comes printed with a design on it, simply wipe with a damp paper towel to remove.*

# ALMOND ROYAL ICING

1 egg white,* at room temperature
2 to 2½ cups sifted powdered sugar
½ teaspoon almond extract

*Use only grade A clean, uncracked eggs.*

**1** Beat egg white in small bowl with electric mixer until foamy.

**2** Gradually add 2 cups powdered sugar and almond extract. Beat at low speed until moistened. Increase mixer speed and beat until icing is stiff, adding additional powdered sugar if needed.

# CHINESE CHECKERS CAKE

*You'll score big with this fun cake.*

## What You'll Need

Candy: jelly beans (10 each of 6 colors to match sugars),
 60 black candy-coated chocolate pieces
1 package (18 ounces) cake mix, plus ingredients to prepare mix
1 container (16 ounces) canned white frosting
Blue food coloring
Food storage bags
Toothpick
Colored sugars (7 different colors)

**1** Grease and flour 12- or 14-inch deep-dish pizza pan. Prepare cake mix, and bake in prepared pan according to package directions. Cool in pan on wire rack 15 minutes. Remove from pan to wire rack; cool completely.

**2** Spread half of frosting over top of cake. Tint remaining frosting with blue food coloring; place in resealable food storage bag. Cut off corner of bag, and pipe large 6-pointed star on top of cake. (First trace out star with toothpick to use as guide.)

**3** Fill each star point with different sugar color. Arrange 10 jelly beans in each star point, matching color of sugar in opposite point. Fill in center of star with last color sugar and arrange black candy pieces as shown in photo.

**4** Apply blue frosting to sides of cake.     Makes 12 servings